McLean's ABC CULTURAL COMPETENCE MODEL

A CULTURALI

SHARON MCLEAN

B W E

McLean's ABC Cultural Competence Model

Published by
Business With Excellence
Surrey
England
www.businesswithexcellence.com

ISBN 978-0-9927360-1-9

Cover design by *Sophos Books.*
Printed in the United Kingdom.

CONTENTS

ACKNOWLEDGEMENTS

I am thankful to my parents, Miriam Lawrence and Herbert Lawrence, of Jamaican heritage, for their tenacity and resilience in demonstrating cultural competency first-hand by coming to a country to live for over 40 years as part of the *Windrush Generation* in the UK.

I am also thankful to my husband, Noel, and my children, for their continuous support and input as I have written this book. I am thankful to my siblings, friends and colleagues who have helped me to embrace culture. Thanks to my clients in the counselling and business arena for giving me the space to support you.

PREFACE

From an early age I have been fascinated by my own culture and the different cultures that I have interacted with. I have been inspired through my personal and working life and found out that there is a depth and richness to cultures. As such, I am convinced that it is important to embrace your own culture first then learn about others to appreciate difference.

This book will take you on a journey where you can hear about my story, be challenged to write your own story about culture. You can use a simple model (the McLean's ABC Model) that I have devised in relation to cultural competence in your life, work, business, and community. This book can be used experientially in relation to race and ethnicity.

There are a range of questions to use for organisations, community groups, counsellors, and individuals to help them to embrace culture.

There is guidance on how to devise your own charter and discussion points to help you delve into the topic at a deeper level.

This book can be used individually, in small groups or part of a training or teaching session.

It is my desire that from using this book you will be confident in being culturally competent.

Sharon McLean (M.A)

MY STORY

The Impact of Culture and Race

After reflecting on five decades of my life and the 2020 George Floyd murder that woke the world again to the evil of racism and systemic discrimination that exists in institutions, I was left asking many questions and experiencing a range of different emotions. I will share my journey below.

My heritage

I am proud of my Caribbean heritage. My parents came to the UK as part of the *Windrush Generation,* which included people arriving in the UK from 1948 onwards. Windrush refers to the ship *MV Empire Windrush* that first docked in Tilbury on 22nd June 1948, bringing workers from Jamaica, Trinidad and Tobago, and other islands to help fill post-war UK labour shortages.

My parents told me that many of their counterparts originally came to work for five years with the intention of returning to their homeland. However, most ended up staying longer, establishing their families, and raising their children in the UK.

Racism was rife in various systems at the time, namely the Police force, Social Housing, and Churches. I remember my parents telling me that when they were looking to rent a room, they saw signs outside the houses saying, "No blacks, no dogs, no Irish." As a consequence, some Black people were forced to rent rooms from each other until they could afford to buy their own houses.

The challenges of purchasing a home were compounded by the reluctance of Banks to offer mortgages or loans, so they set up their own money system called "partners" (pronounced *pardner* in the Jamaican dialect), where a group of people would agree to give a regular sum of money (or hand) to a trusted person (a respected person of the community) on a weekly basis. Every week, one member of the partner system would receive the total amount contributed by all the partners. This is what many of the early black immigrants used as a deposit to purchase their first homes.

Black people were not welcome in the mainstream Churches. So, as a result, many set up their own prayer meetings in their homes. As the number of people attending these prayer groups increased, they rented halls and eventually were able to purchase buildings for their growing congregations. Hence, the lack of acceptance from the White Christian community is what led to the emergence and growth of Black Majority Churches.

Looking back, I cannot believe this happened, but it did. Talking to my parents and people from the Windrush generation, I noticed they had a certain amount of resilience about them. This caused them to persevere in such hostile conditions. It wasn't that they were emotionally immune to the racism, but they were determined not to be deterred in their attempts to purchase their own homes and look after their families, even if it meant they had to work two or three jobs. Till this day, I love to sit and hear their stories and life experiences!

Growing Up

I grew up in a predominately white area in Buckinghamshire. The majority of my friends in Primary and Secondary School were white and very friendly. But in the church that I attended, the majority were black.

I experienced an openness to all cultures and was happy that in the 1980s they introduced the Multi-Cultural Centre where I lived, to celebrate and appreciate the diverse cultures within our community. This brought the community together and enhanced ethnic cohesion among the people. Although I was not called names at school, I witnessed some of my black friends, especially the boys, being called names such as "nigger" and "gollywog," which was outright racist.

I then realised that most white children using these words were being influenced by their white middle class parents. The media did not help at the time because I could not identify with any of the characters on TV. They did not look or sound like me.

I used to watch the TV show, *Grange Hill,* which was a school show. In one episode, one of the black boys was complaining about the names he was being called by white boys at school and one of the girls turned round to him and said, "It is not your fault you are a nig-nog."

There were racist undertones without us even realising back then. Even the dolls I played with were barbies with blonde hair and blue eyes. So, again, very little around me was culturally relevant.

I only began to see the introduction of black dolls for when I had my children.

In school, we were taught history from a very westernised perspective and black history was not included in the curriculum. It was not until I became older and had black lecturers at the university that I started to research my own history and realised that some of the information taught at school was not culturally holistic or even correct.

Far too often, the historical narrative centred around black people's link to slavery. However, while this formed a very painful part of our history, there were also black inventors, activists, role models, black people that fought in the world war that were not mentioned as a suitable subject matter.

The idea that black people were only competent in areas of music and sport was a common stereotype. Therefore, began to use every opportunity that I had to take part in Black History Month to highlight the amazing achievements of black people in various sectors.

Over a period, I started to sense the impact of my teaching in schools, churches, and business. I realised that I loved to inform, educate, and celebrate, something I continue to do on a regular basis. It is also embedded into my work as an integral part of who I am.

Working Life & Family Life

My working career involved roles within financial institutions and working on marketing campaigns. Within my management roles, I experienced racism on a covert basis. Customers would make comments such as, "You look different to the person I thought I was speaking to on the phone." The turning point came when I decided to set up my business mentoring service, as the people that I was meeting in the business industry were mainly white male professionals who had no understanding of the challenges I faced as a black businesswoman.

As I pursued my business venture and despite many obstacles, I was able to help other black businessmen and women who had experienced similar obstacles and barriers to myself because of their colour. I was able to support them from an emotional perspective and also from a friendship level, whilst remaining professional as I could empathise with their stories.

After having my children, I decided to move into a quiet rural area like where I had grown up, due to my love of the outdoors and the countryside. We were met with comments from white neighbours such as, "You are not going to have parties all the time, are you?" "What work does your husband do as I see him leaving the house at different times of the day?"

One neighbour shared with us after a few years that she thought we would be bad for the community. Again, covert racism. After being in the area for over 19 years, the neighbours got to know us as people, and we were able to challenge some of the negative stereotypes they had in their mind. We get on very well now, but it took 19 years!

Dealing with Systemic Racism

Racism is in most systems and forms part of normal practices, but there is nothing normal about it. Ruth King (2018), in her book *Mindful of Race, Transforming Racism from the Inside Out,* suggests it is a heart issue and I would concur.

The following are my thoughts towards how we can deal with systemic racism on an individual level and within organisations.

Individuals

As a Counsellor and Supervisor dealing with a range of different cultures daily, I tend to learn a lot from listening to the stories of my clients and supervisees.

It is important to be honest with ourselves, consider whether we have been a victim of racism, covertly or overtly, and address the issue. It is also important for those who are in pain to have safe spaces and forums to talk about their experiences and share with others.

Not only is it important to be heard but also to have the feeling of being understood. Those who have unconscious biases need to regularly evaluate their personal beliefs, conversations, and practices, as invariably, this will highlight underlying prejudices.

Terms and acronyms used by individuals, such as BAME (Black Asian Minority Ethnic) should be challenged, as it lumps everyone who is not white into a singular category.

We should also avoid statements like, "They are playing the race card" without first investigating the facts as the pain in my experience has been exacerbated by these blanket statements.

Organisations

Behind every organisation or institution there is a system based on and fuelled by ideas and ideologies. These ideologies then form practices. If ideas are racially biased or prejudiced, practices will reflect this. It is important to examine the structure that promotes and facilitates what these systems produce. Unless a system is reformed, it will only produce the same thing it is programmed to produce.

One way to challenge established ideologies is to ask the following questions?

- What does it believe?
- How was it set up?
- Who runs it?

Confronting issues around diversity and inclusion might be an uncomfortable exercise, but it is necessary. The process should involve gaining feedback from staff, which is a useful way to help identify racism within organisations. There are various police reports that have exposed institutional racism, ethnic and racial profiling in organisations. For example, the *Macpherson Report* (1999) highlighted institutional racism with the Police force after the racist murder of teenager Stephen Lawrence.

These things affect presumptions. Unless they are eroded, they will continue to form the basis of the systems.

Representation

Unconscious biases could favour one race over the other, limiting the progress of a particular group of people. If, therefore, a group is poorly represented within a system, a wider consultation process will help bring holistic input into the system where biases can be identified and eradicated.

Representation and wider consultation in an organisation, from the top down, should be prioritised. The emotional, psychological, and physical barriers that black people face through unconscious biases should be addressed.

Blind Spots

It is important for people to acknowledge cultural blind spots or they would end up promoting a system that is racist and not even realise it. In the example of the Johari Window below, there is a blind spot. There must be an openness to hearing or considering what you do not see, but others do.

Some systems where blind spots need to be challenged and changes implemented include the police, judiciary, immigration, health, and education.

The Johari Window

1 Open Known to self and to others	2 Blind Not known to self but known to others
3 Hidden Known to self but not to others	4 Unknown Not known to self or others

(Joseph Luft and Harrington Ingham)

Solidarity

There must also be a sense of solidarity that acknowledges racism as our problem and not just feels sorry for the people affected by it. So, having a 360-degree review where people who are different to us look at the same issue and form or make some statements of commitment on an ongoing basis will foster and enhance solidarity.

Listening

As stated earlier, listening is crucial and we must listen to understand. Tackling racism should form part of the agenda within organisations and not just a one-off tokenism when the issue comes up in the media.

Ongoing learning is important and speaking out with organisations who can rally around, partner with, and support each other shows signs of collaboration.

Our work and training

As counsellors, we can speak with our clients and ask them about the impact of racism within our practice and training organisations. Someone must be available to listen. The process must be legitimate where our voices can be amplified and an opportunity for feedback to be given. This will always keep the issue at the forefront. If racism is maintained on the agenda, especially, in areas of power and influence, then "the elephant in the room" will have to be addressed.

God, Racism and Justice

As a person of faith, I believe we are created in the image of God with different aspects. Every person that God creates has intrinsic value. Anything that undermines or devalues that is an offence to God. Our skin colour should not be a factor that determines how we are treated.

Will you be the change in your area of influence?

Reflection

Note down your initial thoughts after reading my story.

Activity

Now write your own story using the following headings or add your own.

My Story

My Heritage

Growing Up

Working Life

Family Life

Blind Spots

Representation

Reflect on each topic what have you learnt about yourself?

“ Quote for discussion

"Judge me based on who I am and not the colour of my skin." (Reflect and discuss).

“ Quote for discussion

"Racism is our problem and not just my problem, we are in this together." (Reflect and discuss).

Quote for discussion

"Empathise with how I feel, and what I have been through to get a better picture." (Reflect and discuss).

INTRODUCING THE MCLEAN'S ABC CULTURAL COMPETENCE MODEL

Aim

To introduce you to the experiential model and show you how it can be included, expressed, and embraced in your work in relation to culture and race.

This model will help you answer and act upon the following questions:

- How can you include culture in your work and life?
- How can you help others to see the benefits of expressing their culture?
- How can you embrace the experience of culture so it adds value?

What does culture include?

Culture is more attached to certain people and groups, and it is generational. Culture is also something you inherit. Aspects of culture can include the following: our attitudes, beliefs, language, customs, rituals, behaviour, faith, religion, food, art, drama, films, television, and music. Culture is a description of how we express ourselves in these areas.

Take each topic of interest and answer the following questions. You can also ask others.

- What are my/your attitudes to culture?
- What are some of my/your beliefs about culture?
- How do I/you feel about my/your language or dialect?
- What are some of my/your customs?
- What are some of my/your rituals?
- How do I/you like to express myself/yourself as a person?
- How important is faith to me/you?
- What religion do I/you associate with?
- What foods are a representation of my/your culture?
- How do I/you see art in relation to my/your culture?
- How do I/you see drama, film, and television in relation to my/your culture?

- How does music influence my/your culture?

LET'S LOOK AT YOU

When considering culture, the first person to look at is yourself. The following important questions will help us to take this first step of looking inwardly at ourselves and feeling comfortable with talking about our culture. We may have different starting points and it is important to work through our own reflections, feelings, and thoughts before we ask others. Once you have done this activity on your own, you can do it with others.

Where were you born?

Where are your family from?

Where do you trace your ancestry from?

What is your experience of interacting with other cultures?

How comfortable do you feel telling your story about your culture?

How does your culture impact the way you relate to people?

Are there any aspects of your culture that you find embarrassing or difficult to share?

Do you think there are any beliefs or prejudices within your culture that is harmful to others?

Top Tip

After answering the questions, you can discuss with others and share any similarities or differences.

- *What have your learnt about someone else just by listening?*
- *After listening, what will you now do differently?*

WHY IS CULTURE IMPORTANT?

- Culture reflects a community and nation.
- It provides feelings of security and safety.
- Sharing the same history and ideology can connect people to their ancestry and provide a sensation of longevity, which gives a feeling of truth and authenticity.
- Cultural competence in relation to race is very important and dismissing it can be harmful.

Activity

Is Culture important to you? If yes, why?

Culture is important to me because…

WHY CULTURAL COMPETENCE IS ESSENTIAL IN OUR WORK

The Equality Act 2010 sets out nine Protected Characteristics namely:

- Age
- Disability
- Gender reassignment
- Marriage and civil partnership
- Pregnancy and maternity
- Race
- Religion or belief
- Sex/Gender
- Sexual orientation

These protected characteristics are aspects of a person's identity that make them who they are. Any discriminatory behaviour or harassment in relation to these is unlawful. As unique individuals, it is important for us to look at things from different lenses.

Reflection

Think about those you have worked with and reflect on how you have treated people, whether consciously or unconsciously, in relation to the 9 protected characteristics?

Are there things you have done, whether implicitly or explicitly, to impair others?

Now think about how you may have been treated by others in relation to any of the above protected characteristics. How did it make you feel?

Top Tip

We all have blind spots so we must be open and willing to learn and do things in a different way.

Activity

How does your culture impact on any of these protected characteristics? (Reflect, write, or open a conversation about it).

Age

Disability

Gender Re-assignment

Marriage and Civil Partnership

Pregnancy and Maternity

Race

Religion or Belief

Sex/Gender

Sexual orientation

USING THE MCLEAN'S ABC CULTURAL COMPETENCE MODEL

(An Experiential Model)

This model can be used with individuals or groups you encounter. The emphasis is on experiencing the model. It is about incorporating inclusion and diversity into a cultural context and being committed hospitality to all.

There is also the sense of encouraging mutual curiosity regarding the perspectives, knowledge, and experience of everyone present.

The model below depicts an ongoing cycle and flow of experience.

The three cornerstones of the ABC model are *Acceptance, Belonging,* and *Commitment.*

Acceptance is about acknowledging and valuing the individual's or group's different cultural background and experience, and inviting them to speak about their different perspectives. It is not about fitting their experience into your experience, but seeing it from their point of view.

Belonging is about encouraging everyone to feel that they are truly heard, facilitated by an environment where they can share freely and safely; ensuring that their individual perspectives are helpful to the process of learning for everyone.

Commitment is about being determined to explore everything relating to the mainstream content of counselling, training, business, work, and community through the lens of diversity and inclusion on a consistent basis, even if it feels difficult. There is a sense of dedication, loyalty, and responsibility to keep going and address issues that may come to the forefront.

Acceptance

Ask clients, colleagues, or friends to share a visual representation of where they are from. A national flag is a good place to start discussions. You can share what the colours may represent.

Tell your story and get others to tell their story. Listen to stories without coming up with a recommendation or solution. Just hear it from the other person's point of view.

Acceptance Statements

- I value you for who you are.
- I am different from you but that is okay.
- I have parts within me that I like and parts I don't like.
- I will respect what you have to offer.

Have a go at writing your own acceptance statements.

I feel accepted when…

Share with others.

Acceptance Questions

- What does acceptance mean for you?
- How comfortable do you feel sharing your experienced with others?
- If you are uncomfortable, what would make your feel more comfortable?
- What beliefs do you have about yourself that stops you from fully accepting yourself?
- What beliefs do you have about others that will stop you from fully accepting them?

Top Tip

Be honest in your reflections regarding yourself and others.

Belonging

Think about when you are in a group. What things help your sense of belonging?

Belonging Statements

- I feel a part of the group.
- My feelings have been acknowledged and validated.
- I can be myself in the group.
- I have heard what you said, and I respect you even if I don't understand.
- I will try my best to understand you.
- Help me to understand from your perspective.

Have a go at writing your own belonging statements.

I feel like I belong when…

Share with your group.

Belonging Questions

- What does belonging mean for you?
- Do you appreciate my difficulties?
- Do you know what my difficulties are?
- In what ways will you make me feel like I belong?
- What steps can I take to foster a sense of belonging?

Top Tip

Take time to know those in your work, space, or group. Allow yourself time.

Commitment

Commitment is about staying on course to complete what you have intended.

Commitment Statements

- I will listen to understand.
- I will be respectful even if I disagree.
- I am committed to raising awareness of culture.
- I will be open to addressing my blind spots.
- I will keep addressing the issue even if it feels difficult.

Write your own commitment statements.

I feel committed when…

Share with others.

Commitment Questions

- What does commitment look like for you?
- When you are part of a group, how can you tell the group is committed?
- When would you like to change?
- How easy is it for you to commit?
- What are the barriers keeping you from making a commitment?

Top Tip

Being committed is an ongoing process, so take your time and realise it does take work. Be persistent and consistent, and if it feels difficult, do not give up.

SCENARIOS USING THE MODEL

There are different situations in which the McLean's ABC Model would be effective. Using the model, consider how you would deal with the following scenarios and be more culturally competent.

Referring to a group as 'Your People'.

Assuming all black people are from Africa.

When completing a form and an option says 'Other' when asking about ethnicity.

Using the term BAME.

Pronouncing difficult names.

Speaking to people who have different accents.

Observing a group who's colour or gender is different from yours.

What would you change or do differently?

Activity

Please list the emotions you feel when you encounter the following scenarios:

You hear an individual or group referring to another group as 'Your People'.

An individual or group assumes all black people are from Africa.

When completing a form about ethnicity and an option says 'Other'.

You hear a person of a different culture using the term BAME (Black, Asian Minority Ethnic).

You hear a person of similar culture using the term BAME (Black, Asian Minority Ethnic).

Someone does not make the effort to pronounce your name or pronounces it wrongly or shortens a name that they find difficult to pronounce.

Someone treats you differently because you speak in a different accent.

Someone says you are in the ethnic minority.

Someone judges and comments on your accent.

You observe a group who's colour or gender is different from yours.

Activity

Please repeat this activity, asking a colleague, client, or someone you work with and consider where their emotions are similar to or different from yours.

Please list the emotions you feel when you encounter the following scenarios:

You hear an individual or group referring to another group as 'Your People'.

An individual or group assumes all black people are from Africa.

When completing a form about ethnicity and an option says 'Other'.

You hear a person of a different culture using the term BAME (Black, Asian Minority Ethnic).

You hear a person of similar culture using the term BAME (Black, Asian Minority Ethnic).

Someone does not make the effort to pronounce your name or pronounces it wrongly or shortens a name that they find difficult to pronounce.

Someone treats you differently because you speak in a different accent.

Someone says you are in the ethnic minority.

Someone judges and comments on your accent.

You observe a group who's colour or gender is different from yours.

Activity

- Please talk about your specific work as a counsellor, pastoral carer, employee, leader, or manager, and think about areas where you have been or have not been culturally competent. (Feel free to use pseudonym names).
- What could you do to improve?

EXERCISES FOR REFLECTION

- Reflect on your own background.
- Reflect on other cultures you have worked with.
- Share your stories.
- Listen to the stories of others.
- Don't fast track diversity outwardly just so it looks good.
- Work from the individuals frame of reference—What is their world like?
- Work within their context—What is important for them?

WAYS TO EMBRACE CULTURE

There are many ways to embrace culture. Below are some suggestions to consider.

- Take time out to understand how culture influences people in terms of their behaviour, beliefs, and values.
- Be aware of your own cultural conditioning and the tendency to only look at things from your perspective.
- Be considerate, sensitive, and respectful of other cultural and religious beliefs and practices.
- Respect differences.
- Avoid stereotyping.
- Be careful of your use of language and what different words mean for different cultures.
- Commit to ongoing training for yourself, your profession, and the organisation you work within.

- Keep looking for new ways to learn about the different cultures you may encounter.

DIVERSITY DIALOGUE

(Culture in the wider context)

The idea of "Social graces" was developed by Burnham (1992) and Roper Hall (1998) and can be used to critically explore issues of social difference. As you can see below, *culture* is included as one of the critical factors in this framework.

You can pick a title below and curiously enquire about it to open a conversation in a wider context.

Look at the following words below.

Gender

Geography

Race

Religion

Age

Ability

Appearance

Class

Culture

Ethnicity

Education

Employment

Sexuality

Sexual Orientation

Spirituality

The acronym for all the words above is **GGRRAAACCEEESSS** (or simply GRACES).

What stands out for you from the list? What stands out for your clients, those you care for, and those you work with?

Activity

To open a conversation, get your clients, employees, or work colleagues to choose any of the words in the framework and ask them to describe themselves. List the words separately on a piece of paper or, if working online, on a screen, and ask people to pick the ones that apply to them. This will help you to see how culture is perceived in the wider context.

Gender

Geography

Race

Religion

Age

Ability

Appearance

Class

Culture

Ethnicity

Education

Employment

Sexuality

Sexual Orientation

Spirituality.

GGRRAAACCEEESSS

Are there any topics that jump out to you straight away?

Are there any topics that you consider less important to you?

HOW TO MAINTAIN CULTURAL COMPETENCY

There are many ways to develop and maintain cultural competence. Start by building up your own resources and keep adding to the list. Useful resources can include:

- Books
- Articles
- Podcasts
- You tube clips
- Films
- Documentaries
- Handouts
- Pictures
- Interviews
- Focus Groups
- Quotes
- Discussions

It is important that you keep your resources up to date.

Activity

To be culturally competent, please list the following:

Questions I need to ask myself.

Questions I can ask my clients.

Questions I can ask my employer.

Questions I can ask my organisation.

Areas I need to develop in.

Areas I need to be challenged in.

Additional Activities

Think about who has been a major influence in your life?

What attitudes have you inherited from your parents or main caregiver?

What is your way of being?

Do you encourage people to share their stories?

Can you get experience of communities and cultures different to your own?

Do your own research on race.

Think about how the impact of culture plays out psychologically and somatically in their bodies.

Activity

Read the thought-provoking letter by George Yancy on White America, published in the *New York Times* (available at the following link: https://archive.nytimes.com/opinionator.blogs.nytimes.com/2015/12/24/dear-white-america/). Note and share your thoughts about the letter. I will share my reflections as well.

Reflection

What feelings or emotions has this letter evoked in you?

Was it painful to read?

What parts stood out to you?

What will you do differently after reading this?

My Reflections

This letter may be uncomfortable reading for some. However, after ruminating on it, here are a few salient points to consider:

- Is White America ready to confront its racism?
- It is important to speak our truth.
- It is important to own our own issues regardless of our status.
- There needs to be an acknowledgement of failure, engage critically and to challenge assumptions.
- Black women and women of colour have not only been victim of racism but sexism.
- Just because things have been done unintentionally, we must take responsibility.
- There is a vulnerability that we need to have when owning racism and not hide it.
- We must also face our own racist history.
- Parts of racism is systemic.
- There is internalised racism and

institutionalised racism.

- Robert Jensen's comment about walking in a store at the same time as a black man and the security guard left him to shop and follows the black man, he stated in this situation he benefits from White privilege.
- There needs to be an acceptance of racism in ourselves. Masks need to be taken off.
- Martin Luther King was murdered even as he loved.
- Black lives need to be valued.

Quote for discussion

"When confronted with pain, do not run away from it, face it." (Reflect and discuss).

THE POWER IN SPEAKING

Speaking out on issues surrounding culture has many benefits. It can release you from unexpressed thoughts you hold in your mind. Write down the things you need to speak about regarding your culture or questions you may have about culture.

I need to speak about…

I have questions regarding…

The Power of Words

Look at the words listed below. Research their meanings and discuss with examples. What emotions do they evoke in you in relation to culture? (Discuss)

White privilege

Otherness

Microaggression

Equality v Equity

Representation

Examine the groups you work with or belong to. Is your culture represented at all levels?

Leadership Level

Board Level

Management Level

Staff Level

Note your thoughts.

What can be changed?

Reflection

What comes to mind when you hear the following words? (Research and discuss)

Cultural Humility

Cultural Appropriation

Cultural Appreciation

Cultural Sensitivity

Cultural Intelligence

CULTURAL COMPETENCE CHARTER

Devise a Cultural Competence Charter for yourself, your work, or organisation, to include some of the words below of how you will now do things. These can include words from the model such as *Acceptance, Belonging, Commitment, Monitoring and Evaluation.* Fill in the words and statements below. Please feel free to expand on this to make it personal to you.

When writing your charter, it is helpful to acknowledge change, allow time for change, and respect change.

- Acknowledge change.
- Allow time for change.
- Respect Change.

Acceptance

I/We will foster a sense of acceptance by doing the following:

Belonging

I/We will create a sense of belonging by doing the following:

Commitment

I/We will be committed to be cultural competence by doing the following:

MONITORING AND EVALUATION

It is important that organisations monitor and evaluate the level of cultural competence within their workforce and corporate structure. However, monitoring and evaluating cultural competence within an organisation must be more than a tick-box exercise.

- Monitoring has to do with checks and balances within the organisation.
- Evaluation asks the questions: What is good practice? What have we done well? How can we improve?

Using the *McLean's ABC Cultural Competence Model* of Acceptance, Belonging, and Commitment, how can you monitor and evaluate what you are doing to be deemed as Culturally competent?

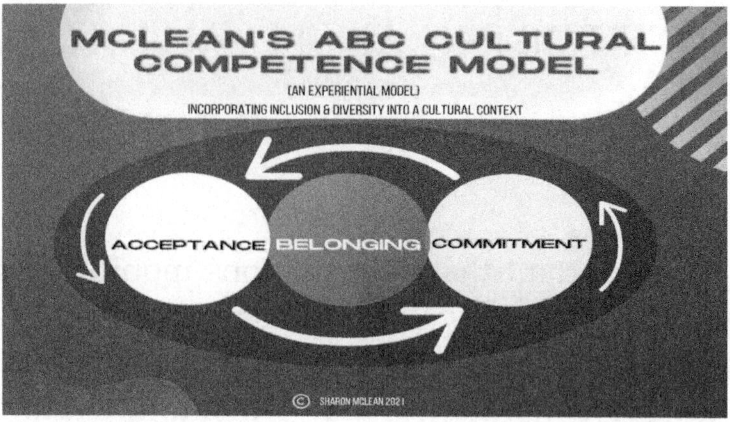

Acceptance

Belonging

Commitment

Questions for Counsellors

- How do I see culture?
- Am I accepting of my client's culture?
- Do I foster an environment where they feel like they belong?
- Am I committed to curiously enquiring about how I can learn more about their culture and what it means to them?
- Am I aware of any blind spots?
- Are there areas I feel uncomfortable talking about?

Questions for clients

- Tell me about your culture?
- Tell me about your ancestry?
- How do you see culture?
- Do you think the difference in our ethnicity could be a barrier in our work together?

Questions for Business Owners

- Is my business culturally competent?
- How do I allow for representation in my work?
- How often do I monitor and evaluate in relation to cultural competence?
- How do I promote diversity and inclusion in relation to culture in my work?

Questions for Pastoral Carers

- Am I accepting of people from a different culture?
- Do I allow them space to share their story?
- Do I make judgements based on a client's culture?
- How well informed am I of the cultures of the people I support?

Questions for Organisations

- Does our organisation function in a culturally competent way?
- How does that look in each area?
- Are a variety of cultures represented at every level in our organisation?
- Are our systems and ways of working culturally competent?

Questions for Churches

- Are we open to a range of cultures?
- Do we celebrate difference and uniqueness?
- Do we represent the culture of our community?
- How can we change things and become more culturally competent?

Questions for the Community

- Are we functioning within a diverse community?
- Are we willing to listen to other cultures?
- Are we willing to learn from other cultures?
- Are we aware of the challenges different cultures may have?

Other Thoughts

If you would like to book Sharon to speak at your event or for training, please email:

info@businesswithexcellence.com

Connect with Sharon

Website:

www.businesswithexcellence.com

Facebook:

www.facebook.com/businesswithexcellence

Twitter:

www.twitter.com/SharonBWE

LinkedIn:

Sharon McLean

Printed in Great Britain
by Amazon

27923798R00056